12/14

frog

OR

toad?

Susan Kralovansky

Consulting Editor, Diane Craig, M.A./Reading Specialist

Super Sandcastle

An Imprint of Abdo Publishing
www.abdopublishing.com

visit us at www.abdopublishing.com

Printed in the United States of America, North Mankato, Minnesota
062014
092014

THIS BOOK CONTAINS
RECYCLED MATERIALS

Editor: Liz Salzmann
Content Developer: Nancy Tuminelly
Cover and Interior Design and Production: Mighty Media, Inc.
Photo Credits: Kelly Doudna, Shutterstock

Library of Congress Cataloging-in-Publication Data

Kralovansky, Susan Holt, author.
  Frog or toad? / Susan Kralovansky ; consulting editor, Diane Craig, M.A., reading specialist.
     pages cm. -- (This or that?)
  Audience: 004-010.
  ISBN 978-1-62403-286-8
  1. Frogs--Juvenile literature. 2. Toads--Juvenile literature. I. Craig, Diane, editor. II. Title.
  QL668.E2
  597.8--dc23
                      2013041845

Super SandCastle™ books are created by a team of professional educators, reading specialists, and content developers around five essential components—phonemic awareness, phonics, vocabulary, text comprehension, and fluency—to assist young readers as they develop reading skills and strategies and increase their general knowledge. All books are written, reviewed, and leveled for guided reading, early reading intervention, and Accelerated Reader® programs for use in shared, guided, and independent reading and writing activities to support a balanced approach to literacy instruction.

contents

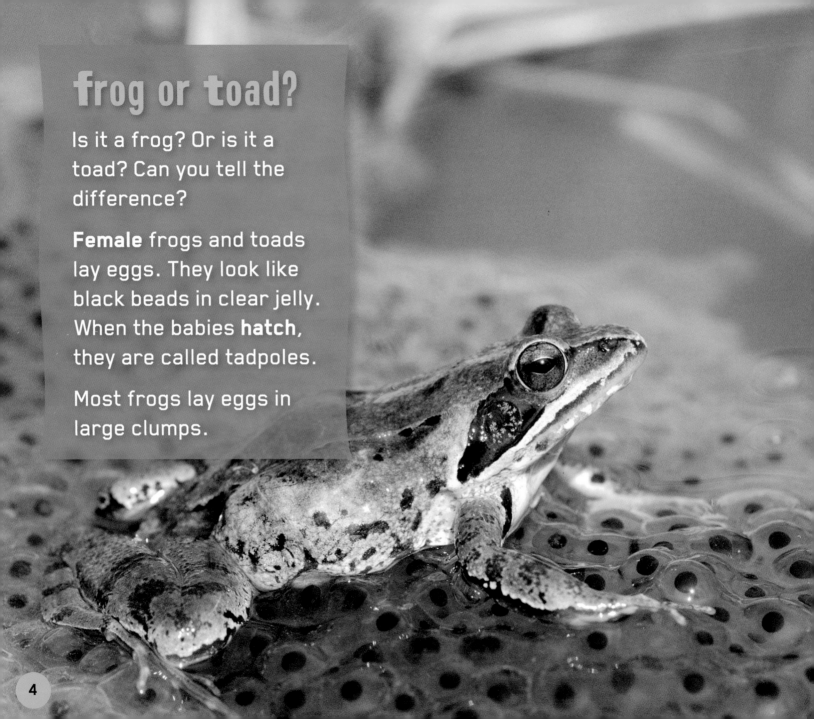

frog or toad?

Is it a frog? Or is it a toad? Can you tell the difference?

Female frogs and toads lay eggs. They look like black beads in clear jelly. When the babies **hatch**, they are called tadpoles.

Most frogs lay eggs in large clumps.

Toads usually lay eggs in long strings.

tadpoles, not fish

Frog and toad tadpoles look like fish.
They don't have legs. They have tails.
They swim around eating plants.

Tadpoles breathe with **gills**. As they get older, their tails and gills disappear. They grow legs.

bright or brown?

Frogs can be dull or brightly colored. Some brightly colored frogs are also **poisonous**.

Most toads are dull brown or gray. This helps them hide in trees and mud.

smooth or bumpy?

Frogs have wet, smooth skin. Their skin makes a **slime** that keeps it **moist**.

Frogs breathe air through their **lungs**. They also take in **oxygen** through their skin.

Toads have dry, bumpy skin.
The bumps are special **glands**.
The glands make poison.

This poison causes the skin to taste bad. Predators soon learn to leave the toads alone.

no chewing!

Frogs and toads eat **insects** and small fish. They catch them with their tongues. Then they swallow the **prey** whole.

Frogs have very small teeth on their upper **jaws**. They use their teeth to hold prey.

Toads do not have teeth. They must swallow their **prey** quickly.

leap or hop?

Frogs have short front legs. They have long, strong back legs. Frogs can leap several times their body length. This helps them hunt and escape from predators.

Toads also have short front legs. Their back legs are shorter than frogs' back legs. Toads walk or make short hops along the ground.

at a glance

frog ——————————————————— toad

lays eggs in a clump ————————— lays eggs in long strings

dull or brightly colored ————————— dull colored

wet, smooth skin ————————— dry, bumpy skin

have very small teeth ————————— do not have teeth

able to make long leaps ————————— walks or makes short hops

tp roll frog craft

your friendly frog has smooth skin and long, leaping legs.

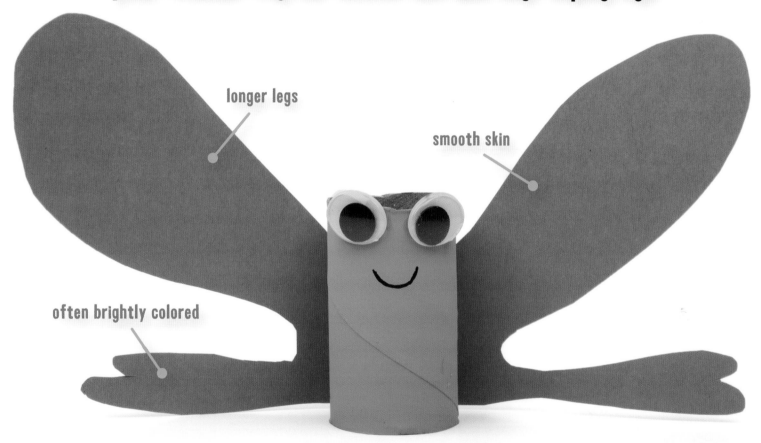

longer legs

smooth skin

often brightly colored

What You'll Need
- toilet paper roll
- scissors
- green paint (tempera or acrylic craft paint) and brush
- green construction paper or card stock
- pencil
- googly eyes
- glue
- black marker

1 Cut off the top third of the TP roll. Paint the remaining part of the roll green. Let the paint dry.

2 Place the TP roll on the green paper. Draw frogs' legs coming up each side with a pencil. Add long feet.

3 Cut out the pattern. Your frog's legs should look like the picture.

4 Cut two **slits** in the TP roll about 1 inch (2.5 cm) apart. Make the slits about 2 inches (5 cm) long.

5 Slide your frog's legs into the slits. The feet should be even with the bottom of the roll.

6 Glue on two googly eyes. Draw a friendly frog smile!

tp roll toad craft

your friendly toad has bumpy skin and short, hopping legs.

shorter legs

bumpy skin

dull or brown in color

What You'll Need

- toilet paper roll
- scissors
- small bowl
- potting soil
- brown paint (tempera or acrylic craft paint) and brush
- brown construction paper or card stock
- pencil
- googly eyes
- glue
- black marker

1 Cut off the top third of the TP roll. Mix a little dirt and brown paint together. Paint the remaining part of the TP roll and one side of the brown paper. Let the paint dry.

2 Turn the paper over. Place the TP roll on the unpainted side. Draw thick toads' legs coming up each side with a pencil. Add long feet.

3 Cut out the pattern. Your toad's legs should look like the picture.

4 Cut two **slits** in the TP roll about 1 inch (2.5 cm) apart. Make the slits about 2 inches (5 cm) long.

5 Slide your toad's legs into the slits. The feet should be even with the bottom of the roll.

6 Glue on two googly eyes. Draw a friendly toad smile!

23

glossary

female – being of the sex that can produce eggs or give birth. Mothers are female.

gill – the organ on a fish or tadpole's side that it breathes through.

gland – an organ in the body that makes chemicals that the body needs.

hatch – to break out of an egg.

insect – a small creature with two or four wings, six legs, and a body with three sections.

jaw – one of the two bones in the face that teeth grow out of.

lung – an organ in the body used for breathing air.

moist – slightly wet.

oxygen – a colorless gas found in air, water, and most rocks and minerals.

poisonous – able to injure or kill when touched or eaten.

prey – an animal that is hunted or caught for food.

slime – a slippery, soft substance.

slit – a narrow cut or opening.